This Book Belongs To

_____

_____

This Book Belongs To

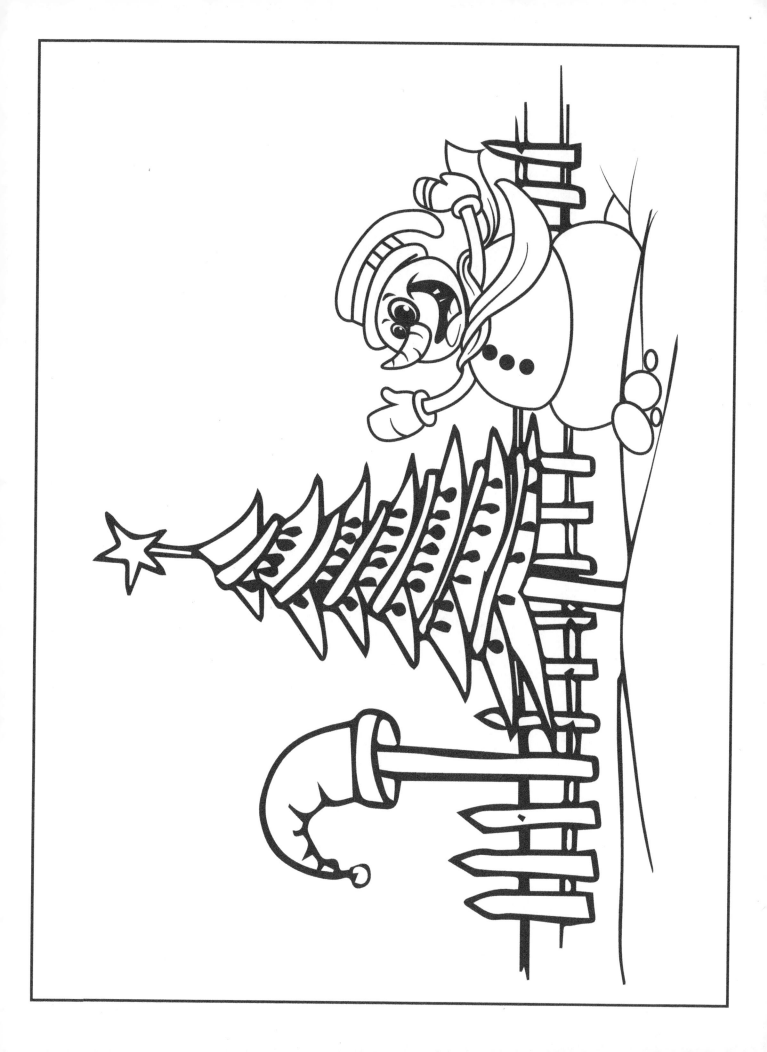

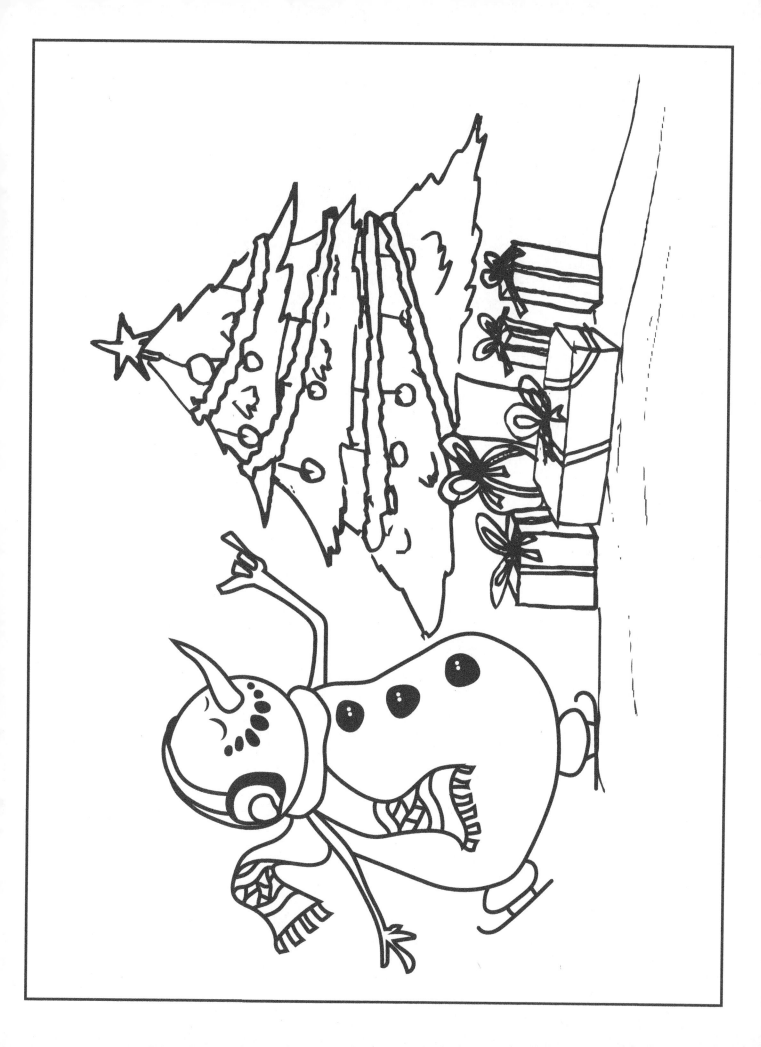

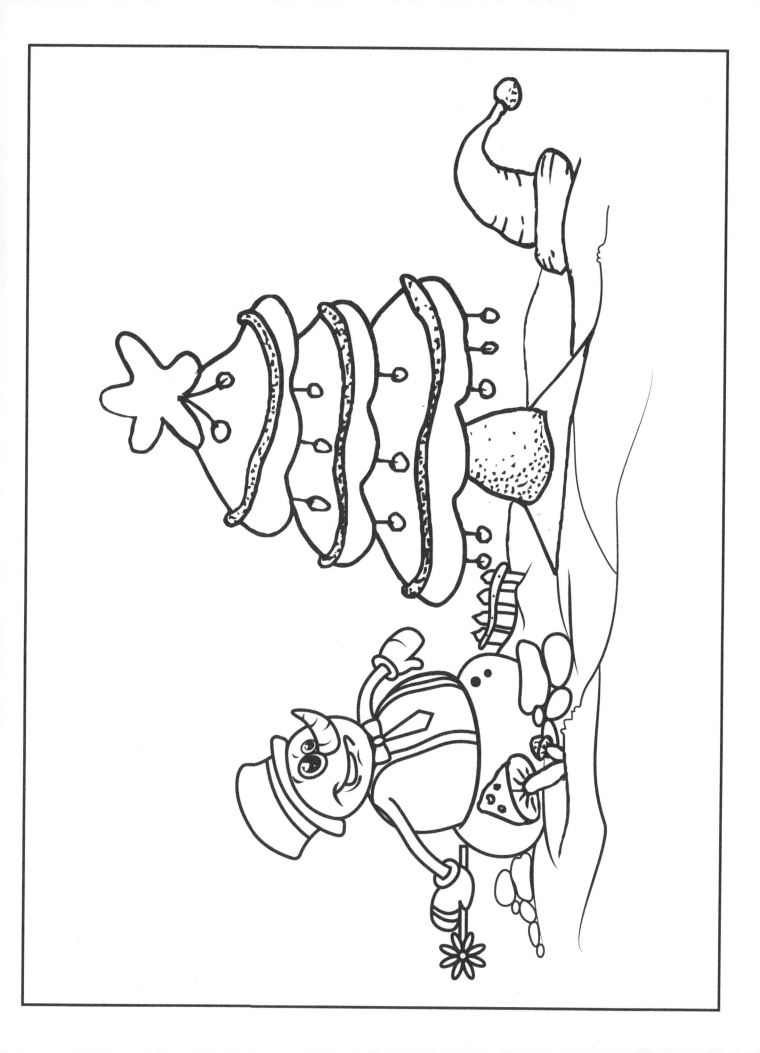

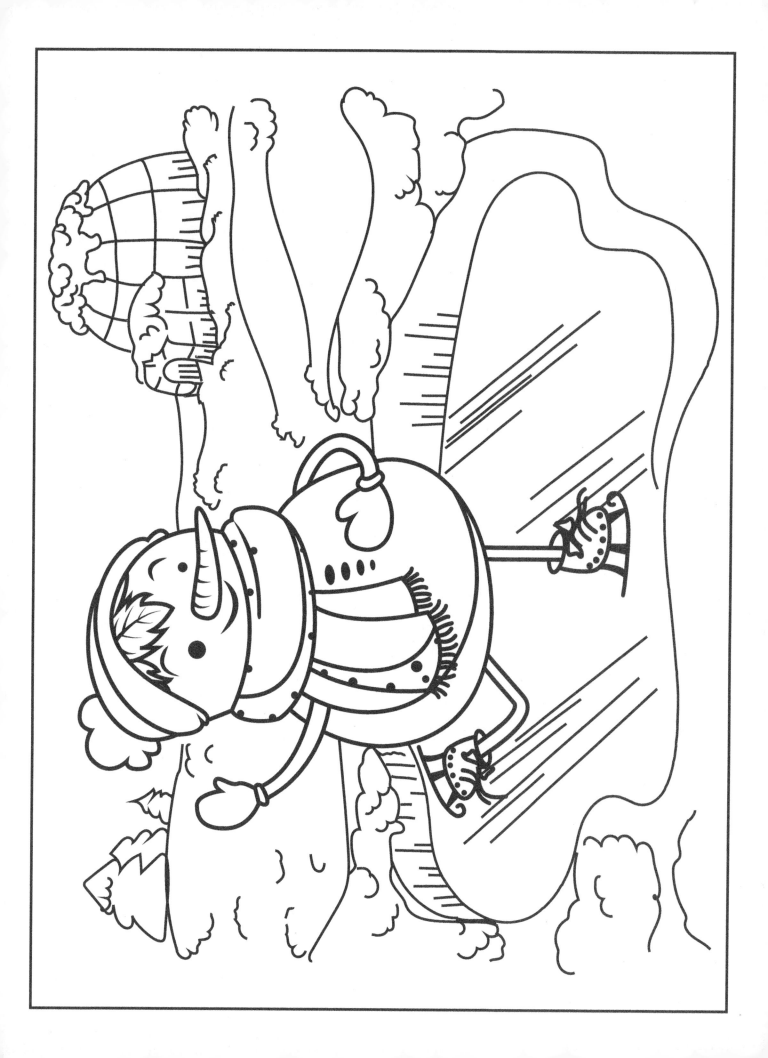

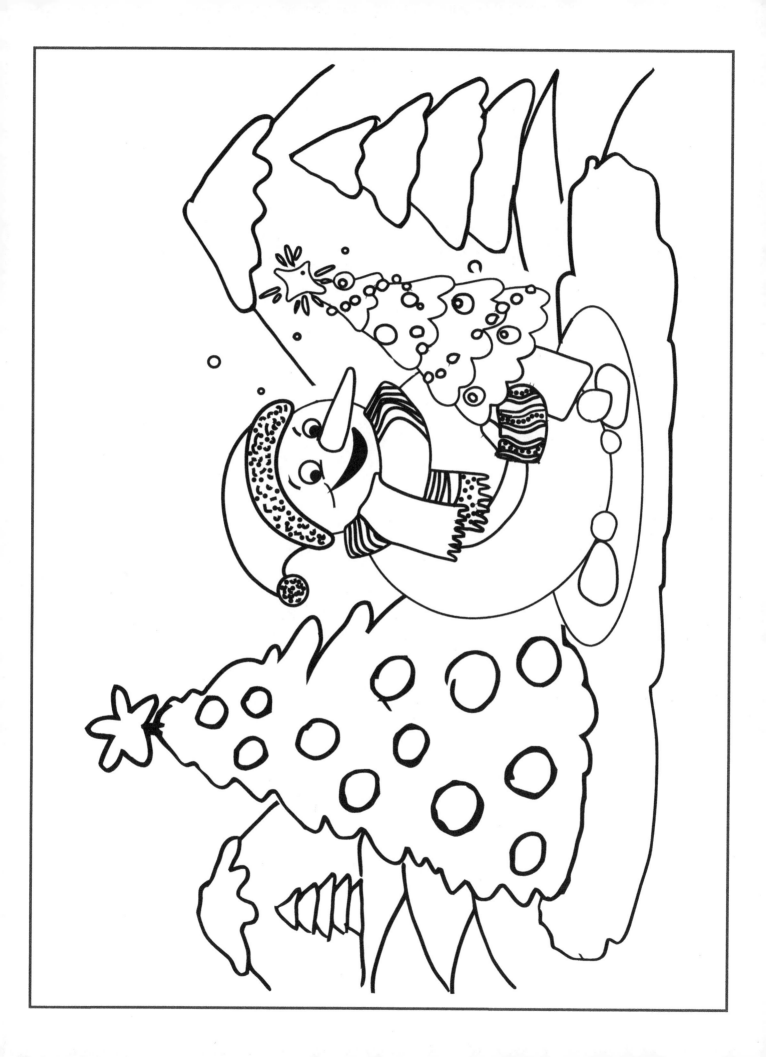

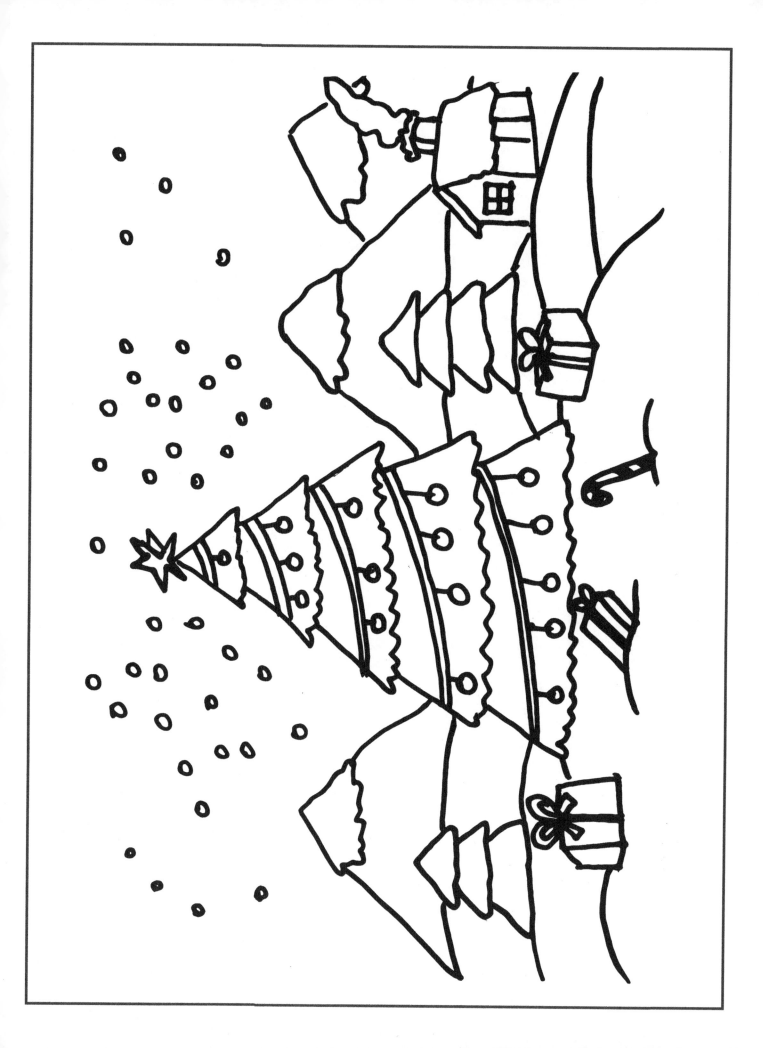

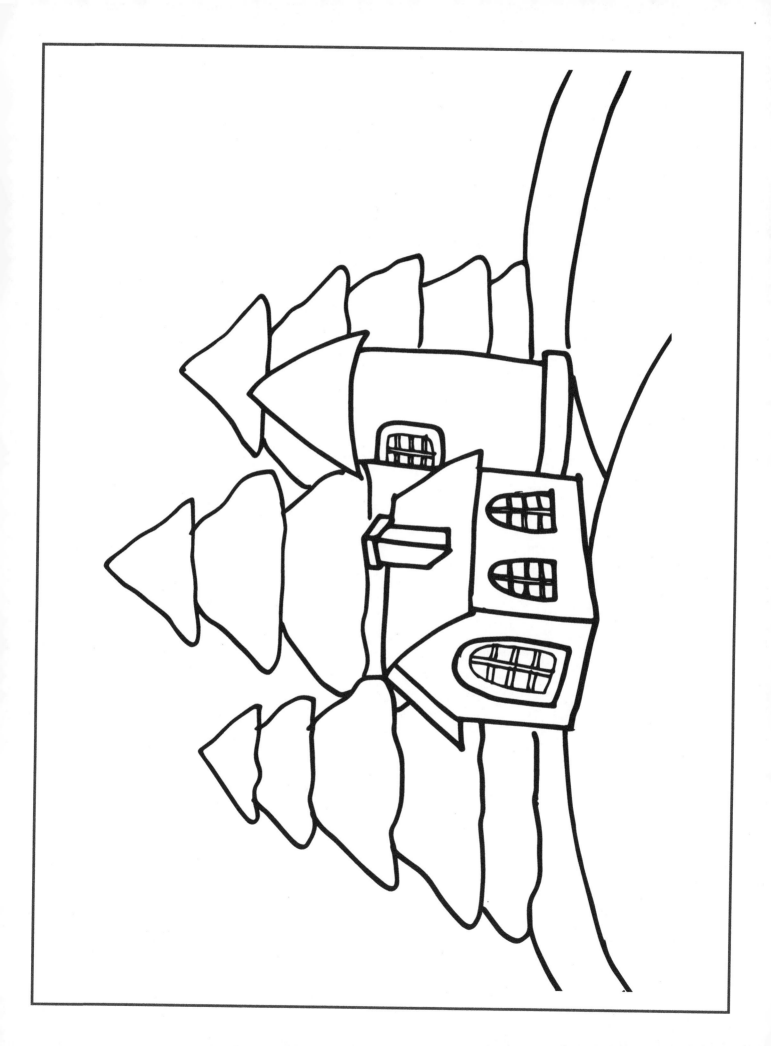

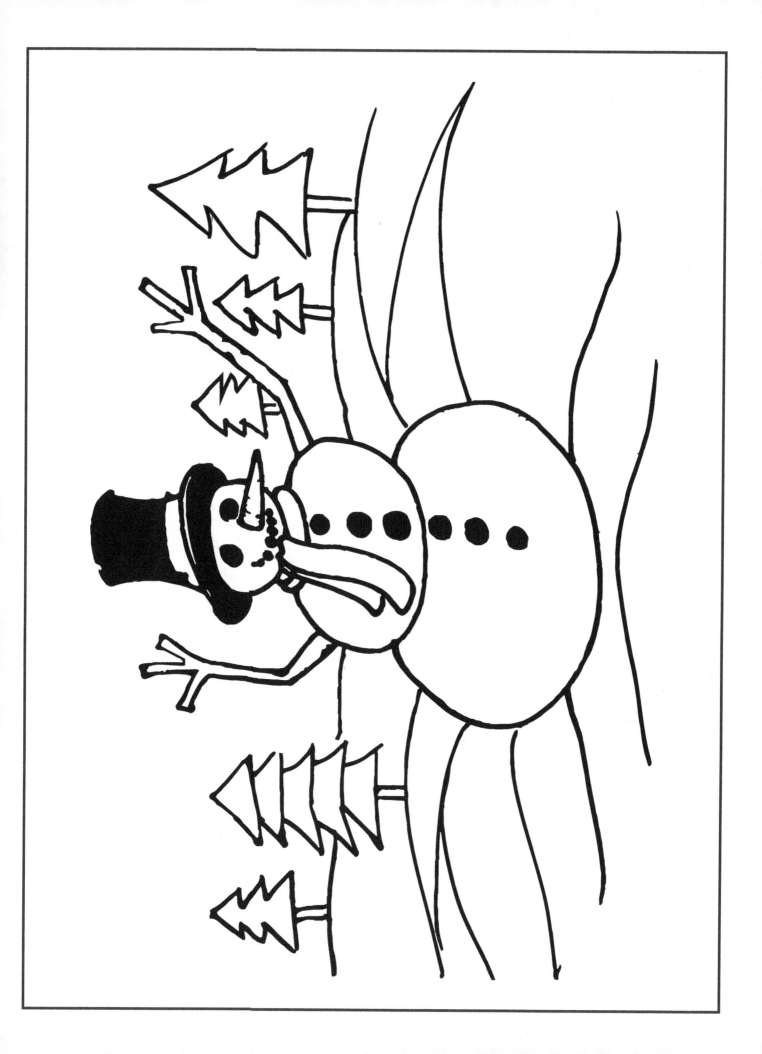

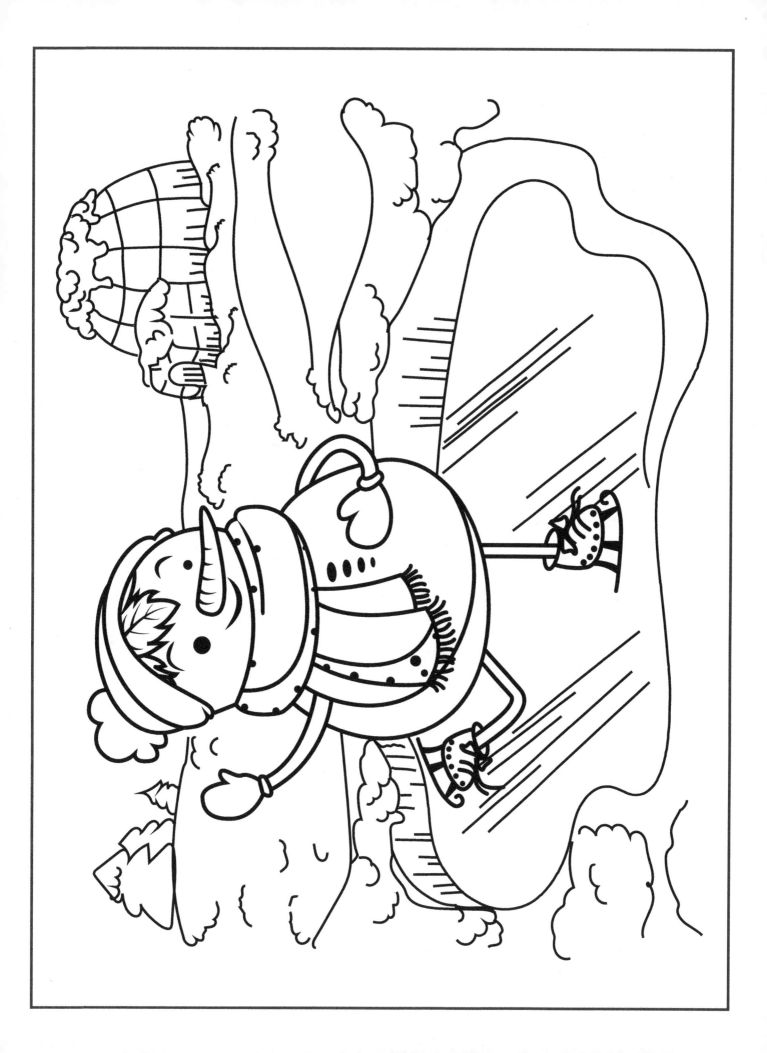

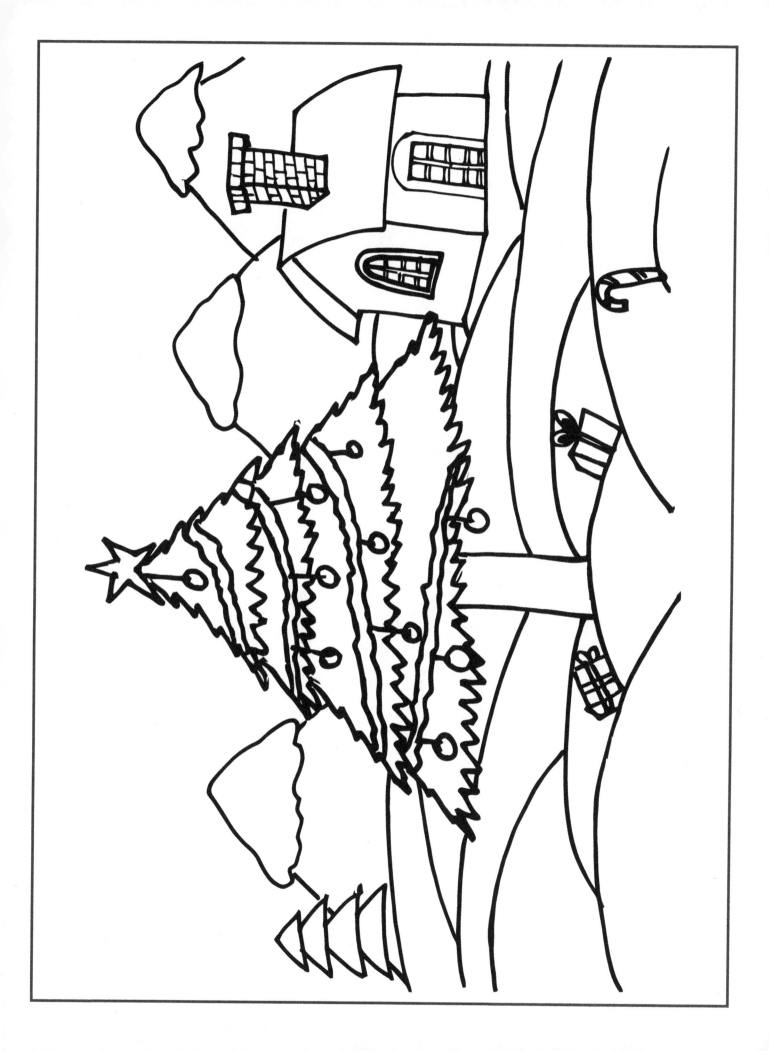

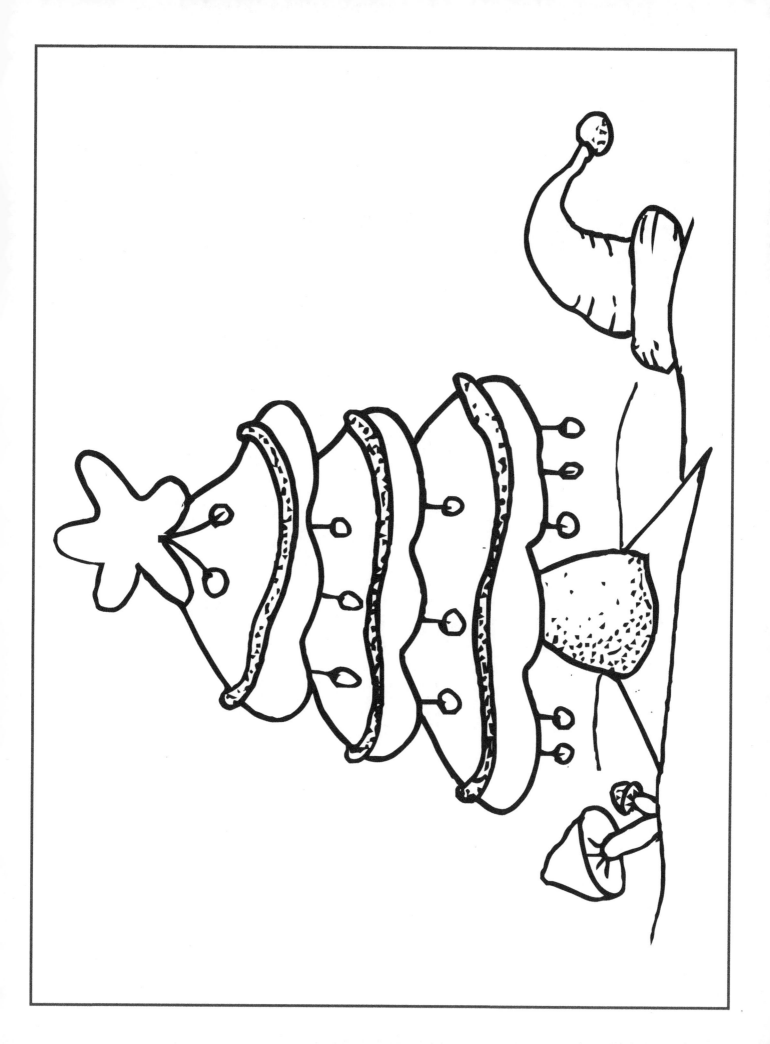

From the Author

From the bottom of our hearts, we really want to thank you for buying this coloring book and sincerely hope that you liked it!

We are truly happy in helping people through publishing books and to know your opinion is really a big help for us to improve.

We would really appreciate if you could leave a review!

Thank you!

Maky Publishing

For more Maky Publishing books visit our Amazon store
and follow us on our social media accounts for updates!

Amazon

YouTube

Facebook

Instagram

Made in the USA
Middletown, DE
04 December 2024